MOTIVETRY

All for Life

SUDEEPTO MISHRA

 pencil

ISBN 978-93-5458-558-6
© SUDEEPTO MISHRA 2021
Published in India 2021 by Pencil

A brand of
One Point Six Technologies Pvt. Ltd.
123, Building J2, Shram Seva Premises,
Wadala Truck Terminal, Wadala (E)
Mumbai 400037, Maharashtra, INDIA
E connect@thepencilapp.com
W www.thepencilapp.com

Author biography

Sudeepto Mishra, also known as Sudeep is an Industrial Design Engineer, an Entrepreneur, a proprietor by profession in his late 20s hailing from the city of temples. Since his class 8th, he has received many prizes and awards in the field of writing at the high school and college levels. Having completed his bachelor's in Mech. Engineering in 2015, he has contributed many of his writings to the university magazine.

As a free thinker and an artist, he tries to express his views with subtleness in discrete genres of poetry and stories. His scribbles pop up as the first preference in any search engine under the title" Just my way to spoil the ink". Many of his works are published in national anthologies and online magazines. He aspires to put more of his writings to the mainstream of mass media and be uniquely visible. He is currently working on his upcoming success and is very passionate to score a home run in this field soon.

Follow Sudeepto -
@https://www.facebook.com/sudeep.mishra.92

Visit the passionate blogger -
https://sood33p.blogspot.com/

CONTENTS

Preface

"No one is actually living without a factor of motivation – be it direct or indirect, enlightened or hidden."

This collection of poems 'Motivetry' is a guiding light to you. If you're down, you're low, you're sad, depressed, confused or you're simply going through rough pensive moods, this is the book for you. This collection is meant to bring back your power and strengthen your inner voice and soul more than before. The ramblings of a broken man will let you relate and feel more powerful as you go through each piece of the poem.

Sometimes, all you need is a person to hold your hand and say that everything would be okay. I'm that person here. Every rhyme and rhythm here speak loudly to get up and walk. There's always a golden stick waiting for you to hold it during your much needful phases. Yet, it is not always visible. You need to find it with a torch which, I believe, this poetry collection acts like.

A rather bitter-sweet phase of a man is captured here to guide others – not to avoid falling into the pit but to get up as soon as possible and keep moving, be ready for the upcoming pits and chances to hold. Life is a multitude of struggles. You can't escape life, but you can certainly escape the unwanted misery and thoughts to give up. You will have to start looking for second chances, third meetings, and fourth luck.

To cheer up souls and fill minds with motivation, Motivetry is a humble attempt for common people, who read, relate, explore and rise.

8

Dedication

FOR MOM AND DAD - FOR ALL YOUR LOVE AND CARE.

To the reader...

Being a motivational catalyst is rare in this self-centric world. I believe we can conquer depression and death with words. We just have to cling and grip firm to it. After all, why fear and live when we don't really know the exact definition of death?

I remember sitting in some dark corner of my room and still writing this line -
"Well, perhaps the thirst might have died. But I am still alive. Still counting."

A long way to go...

There is a long way to go
To count the infinite and so...

There is a lot to seek
With no fears and grief.

Let the time to ooze
For we are ready to cruise,

Jumping the hurdles,
Hopping the puddles.

Putting the arms on
Marching to the battle zone,

To protect the hood,
And to spread the good.

Join the hands strong,
To keep the fence long.

To archive the victory blades
In the chronicles of time thread.

There is a long way to go
To count the infinite and so…

Nature's Express

I thrive for the quest
Diving deep in my thoughts,
The essence of life being happiness
Echoed my ears, that subdues the most.

Beholding the broken sleep,
I stared at the cracked roof,
Looked up at the vast sky
Reflecting the truth.

The crescent moon behind the clouds
Fading out due to unwanted shrouds.
Minutes later the shyness is gone,
And gone are the tangles encountered seldom

The mirror of the sun, translating the pun,
A smile on my face clearing all my stress
Completely satisfied a thousand times
With nature's express.

The Bloodless Sand

Dunes of romantic memories languish with altering winds,
Sand fills the moist eyes; composes a drought in the optic
twins.

Deep urge of restoring love looks like a mirage on the
deserted screen,
Fragments lost in the ocean grit leaving traces of entropic
ruins.

The broken boulevard in the arid zone where the cactuses
throng,
Vagrants plod in search of aqua for the hell of a lifelong,

There I subsist in the radiant scorch and will forever stay,
With a narrow hope of the red sky turning to grey.

My skins have mutated to a tough shell with few scars and
creases,
The fairness quotient has got numbers as the swarthy
bandit ceases,

The well of amour was left un-watered due to a desiccant
of the brawl,
The seekers of the past run into the future to feel the
drawl.

However, I endeavor to plow the sleek bad land,
Earthing a seed of emotion in the bloodless sand...

Touch the core

A source of light is favored from far.
It reflects the outer periphery
Full of efficacy but fatal inside.
The nearer you approach
The more burnt you are.
Life is selfish, death is not,
The core is cold but to cross the frontier
You may evaporate.

An Illusive Dream

In my illusive dream
Fur weighs more than a rock
Falling down to the solid sky,
Beneath the soil, where lonely birds lie.

Moon glows brighter than the solar
Radiating a frozen pale blue flash.
Children play in the pitch dark
Above the clusters of twinkling stars.

The flowers cuddle ugliness,
soaking honey from bee's sting.
Trees are painted viola
leaving no traces of green.

In this bizarre world,
Politicians are dead,
Tribunals are wrecked, peacekeepers on world tours
With luggage full of tin coins and bread.

There's neither a king nor a queen.
Every thought is free to fall
neither gravity nor any other force
can stop its lively soul.

Enigmatic Success

I fear what I am becoming for now,
Confused sometimes and sometimes so strong,
Bamboozled quite often, so fragile in front and back,
Moments later waves of patience waggle my immature
deck.

I see straight lines webbing into puzzles
And convolution drawing simplicity.
I seek for tinder thick and fast
Rather the thirst pleases my ambiguity.

Peace is very nice to cuddle,
But battles I love the most!
Few pieces of stones for me,
And diamonds to others feats and roasts.

That's what I deeply seek for,
My beat is done but don't break yours.
Follow my words and not my turns,
If you cling to it, your heed has a chance.

Never fear death, let it fear you,
Let thy burn and you get the blue.
Your fulfillment may soothe my core,
My blood is gone, your grey matters the most.

My success in disguise is the dream of yours,
Durable are my failure piling lessons to endorse.
A master spell is effective to ponder the triumph,
Find the questions and answers written around.

Motivetry

Rays of hope are penetrating the morning torpor,
Annihilating the junks and stagnancy,
Alarming to worry no more.

Stop the snoozing and put your best foot on the floor.
Ring the bell of happiness with smiles and décor.

Get out of the arranged bricks to replenish the blue sky,
Refresh the nature with your fragrance and comply.

Make a run to wake up the latent heat.
Greet new people and pass the delicious treat.

Witness the wingiers fly so high,
Retweet them and uncage yours into the sky.

Change the sorrows by surpassing the love,
Motivate others, no matter how steep is the curve.

Hold the thought, fueling the will in you
After the night passes, a new morning is in the queue.

Connect the core with melodies and strings of joy.
Replay it again and again to win hearts not toys.

Tulku, The Living Buddha

Thou shall cultivate the ability to feel it all,
Unbound of positive or negative scrolls.
Thou shall connect thy inner intellect,
Improvising awareness of thy current mindset.

Thou shall recognize the curves of thy thoughts,
Unhesitant to discriminate and reframe the plot.
Thou shall put efforts to bypass the subconscious barriers,
Meditating to attain the routes of conscious carriers.

Thou shall volunteer to be everyone's aid,
Impacting the surrounding and selfish trade.
Thou shall preach the essence of humanity,
Bestowing kindness and ultimate world peace.

Irony of life

He looked up at people around
and smiled at their sympathetic looks
They were walking on branded shoes
And he was on wheels.

I stand

I struggle not a single drop to fall
but your tranquility breaks it all.
I hassle to shut my fickle lids
but wayward they pretend and sleep seldom
frightening me up, awakening me so deep.

As if a thick nail hammered to my chest
Rusting slowly decaying me to death.
As if someone choking me off to crave
But there's an ample amount of air
and so is the white keeping me brave.

Can't she feel my ceaseless torment
stabbing me to bleed with so persistence.
It seems extremely hard to hold my pen
even though I live to dip, feel, write
and spoil my ink in her name and fame.

My hands shivering, stammering are my words
but the firm is my legs and so are my roots.
Tall as a mountain I stand with patience
Trying hard not to bend again,
Not to bend again, stronger I stand.

Yesterday's Fog

Yesterday's fog still shivers my rusty soul,
Dauntless seldom intimidating my usual chores.

Shall I adhere to it or let it go,
It is hard to figure out what am I looking for!

It is hard to ponder my next right foot,
Ruthless, rugged shall I be to catch it all.

Grasping, holding my rooted droll
I try to have it and have it all.

A corridor awaits after every next door,
I have to walk alone on the imprints of,
Holding the flambeau of my primitive lore.

The lifeboat

Emerging from the pacific of troubles,
It is the Everest of joy.
Strewed over the bed of thorns,
It is the blanket of coy.

Nullifying the torrents of defeats,
It is the sail of the triumph.
Quenching the castaway of thirst,
It is that drizzle of the oomph.

Obliterating the melancholy of loneliness,
It is the harmony of fulfillment.
Amidst the harrow of the wreckage,
It is the perspective of enlightenment.

Saving lives at the death door,
Is its precious application.
It is the lifeboat,
And this is its definition.

Tale of the Universe

Gigantic world of an unknown master,

Drowning in the drops of the materialistic cluster,

Stabbing nature every possible second
Dwelling in the illusion with no sense to mend,

Framing the fact as a superstition
Making the planet an unreal destination.

Hallo of the unvisited universe calling to claim its rue,
Soon shall face the doom; only lights will remain as a clue.

Expedition to be set for the count,
The beauty of undiscovered realms will beat the sound.

Creatures in the age of extinction will be saved;
Cultures and folks yet to be known are to be engraved.

May there be an advanced intellect governing in stealth,
Might be the almighty god protecting his wealth,

There is a lot to discover and a lot to recall
Strong adherence and determination will answer it all.

Big is the universe and yet more bigly is its tale,
Millions of bytes are needed to record its anabasis sail.

27

And this is life!

What the world is, can somebody say?
Can somebody bring back the memories of my childhood
days?

Bygones by, the time bolts faster than all,
Knitting the cloth of reality with li'l spaces and a li'l bit of
souls.

Maturity neither corresponds to knowledge nor age.
True life experiences break, twist, bend the life to inject it
phase by phase.

Who am I

Who am I, I am I!
I am the lover of my life; I hate my life to death.
I am the hurdle of my decisions; I support my actions and predictions.
I am the maker of my success; I am the reason for my failure.
I am my strongest enemy; I am my best friend.
I am always positive, But negative attracts me the most.
I am my worst critique; I am my biggest fan.
I understand myself the most, I ignore myself almost.
I dare myself to be brave; I fear it never has to crave.
I call myself the hero; Villains are not always at zero.
I like to be me; myself is never what I plea.
Who am I; I am I!

It's something we all will agree on. Each line is true to the best of its construct. Everyone must have thought this at some point in their life span and this is what makes it all very special.

A cup of world

The universe and its tale
Has existed since the big bang
We are perhaps
The first species
To feel and record
Its indegenous vastness
And there is, however,
A lot more to unfold
For here's my notion
If you mix hell and heaven
In a cup,
Our world is formed.

Ponder Positive

The doors will be knocked by the boon
The doom will keep scratching the wound
But persistent is my will
That glows bright in the dark
Neither the largest shadow
Nor the whirlpool of conundrum
Coul divert my perennial path
Stiff are my stances -
Bending negatives to fall
First of my honesty -
Pounding inhuman monsters back to hell.

The best version

Stand for your values
Protect your virtues
For the fame without dignity
Shall be an empty,
False projection of the reality
You're here not to lure
Or attract eyes and minds
But to lead your life
In the best possible way
To be the best version of yourself
Not only to improve thyself
But enhance the fellow passengers.

Subjects in rhythm

I look at the stars in terms of physics,
When I reach them, I find chemistry,
Biology in them is a complete mystery.
When I get more closer, I write poetry,
And then I return to create history.

Run like Milkha

To live his life,
A kid started his run.
The bleeding father,
Put him in command.

Never look back,
Unless you are done.
Go through like bullets,
You are born to run.

He faced many obstacles,
He faced deadly fears,
And was slapped for a blazer,
There was nobody to cheer.

Life was do or die,
Nano-seconds were counted.
On the tracks of thorns and lies,
Each step was accounted.

Once the soil of Pak,
Witnessed his bolstering bolts,
Nicknamed him The Flying Sikh,
Which later became a cult.

Many golds of honor,
glorified his wide chest.
Myriads of records,
Lauded him as the best.

Newbies should draw inspiration,
And must remember his feat.
He was the ideal warrior,
Who never stopped his feet.

He may not be here,
but his deeds are alive.
He ran like Milkha,
Uplifting the Nation's pride.

May

May my words ripple through time,
May I live in the brain of the primes,

Recurring in every dimensionality,
May my soul be felt in every paradigm.

May my vision be sharper,
Sharper than the sharpest,

May I cut through the hardest obstacle,
As effortlessly as the swiftest.

May the truth run in my veins,
In my nerves, my neurons, and my sense.

May honesty be my recognition,
And courage my identification.

May nobility be my aura,
Replenishing Earth's fauna and flora.

May I rip off the shell of the lie,
Spreading truth all over and comply.

Crosses, curves, and lines may trail my traces,

Sentinels, guardians, and angels may gather my pieces.

May there be an equilibrium,
Synchrony in the quotas of deaths and births.

May I equally live and die,
On the surface of the cosmic Earth.

Unmask it all!

Unmask your real face, unravel it all.
Scrap off the thick plastic contrasting face and soul.
Stop drinking potions of Duplicity, call it to an end.
Suffer the thirst of purity, gain the guts to stand.

Miracles are mere, rare is the truth.
Follow the path of whiteness, taming the dark mammoth.
Makeup, manmade beauty has no uniqueness of its own.
Go natural completely with love, fairness, and glow.

Beautiful is the butterfly and so is an almiqui,
With equal opus and heed, nature bestowed its hue.
Discrimination is not the word of almighty,
Nor the virtues of Gods.

He created the universe appointing proper roles,
Smiting intricate caricatures writing distinctive codes.

Burn till your last breath

Burn till your last breath,
you are ought to burn.
Be the scorching radiance,
Blaze like the biggest sun.

When you fall from the heaven
taste the darky swamp.
Let the thorns pierce your chest,
never opt to dump.

Let the red flow from your toiling nerves
Dare not lessen it with a concessive mood.
Salty is the drop of tears and sweat,
Let them fall on the bleeding wound.

Feel every ache and agony.
like every single furrow scattering.
Don't count fingers and toes,
Unite abandoned hearts flattering.

As you accept the tender tales,
embrace the hate with the same zeal.
Forgetting zillions of complaints
Heed one piece of advice as to the biggest deal.

Without diving into suspicion,
Try to introspect and retrospect.
Leaving the act of action,
struggle to build the arrant respect.

Conglomerating heart and mind,
distinguish the same goal.
Imprisoning your instability,
unleash the wisdom scroll.

What is in your name!
Let your deeds identify your stature.
Without rating your difficulties,
Keep roaring like the apex predator.

Inherit the strength from the king of kings,
Dare not to dethrone your pride.
Neither deceit nor malice in your heart,
weaponize your sweat to fight.

By chanting the mantra of justice,
capacitate the feeble yet ready army.
Fill your stomach with earnestness,
Give up on your lazy karmic.

Let the troubled path be cleaned,
By your propaganda of truth.
Burn till your last breath,
combat like an eternal mammoth.

Essence of Life

Breath of the past are still in the atmosphere,
Diffusing the odor of the evil.
Yet the density of the good is heavier,
Spreading the fragrance of free will.

Pondering hopes to innocence,
The sunrays decay the doom,
May it be the cradle or the graveyard,
The starlight nurtures the life to bloom.

Exceptional zeal to grow and thrive,
Undeniably shapes the reverie.
Even void is space yet to explore,
Absolute nothingness is imaginary.

Puny is the mind and heart,
That divides the rich and the poor.
Real weightage vectors humanity,
Strictures of constructivism abide no more.

Ranks and beliefs are temporary,
Space-time changes are the only permanent,
Insipid perspective is probationary,
Probes of empiric only pick the signal evident.

The span of lies is provisional,
Likely to be changed in the future.
The River of truth is perennial,
Is flowing and will flow in nature.

You Keep Doing!

People will see, You keep Doing!
People will say, You keep Doing!
People will discourage, You keep Doing!
People will obstruct, You keep Doing!
People will stop, You keep Doing!
People will change, You keep Doing!
People will learn, You keep Doing!
People will praise, You keep Doing!
People will idealize, You keep Doing!

No matter what, people will always be there, but it's your doing that changes their opinion.

43

You are a Hero

When you fight for the right,
You are a Hero.
When you are afraid of quitting,
You are a Hero.
When you celebrate your failures,
You are a Hero.
When other's grief becomes more valuable than your cries,
You are a Hero.
When you forgive your biggest foe,
You are a Hero.
When you find the enemy inside of you,
You are a Hero.

Fragmented harmonies

Let's run for something
More rudimentary and permanent
Rather than for limited means
Over-exaggerated options
Urging the youth
To follow a perennial path
Because the temporaries
Will fall and lapse
As fragmented harmonies.

What does a wanderer seek!

He smiles and greets the passersby without any hesitation.
Unknown of his own address, he helps voyagers find their
destination.

Belonging to all yet none to call his own,
He roams streets and streets in search of the never-made
clone.

He witnesses the sharp and blunt side of the crude,
Some are full of kindness and others seem a little rude.

He looks at nature's roof expecting the raindrops to fall,
Unaffected by others' thoughts he constantly spreads
happiness among all.

Looking at the sky in search of rainbows, he mimics the
voices of nightingales,
Matching his steps with the rays of Sun he finds shades to
lose the tiredness entangled.

Seeking the moon amidst the clouds he feels the silence of
the dark.
With no clock and a couple of watch-less wrists, he listens
to the ticks of the stark.

Admiring his invisible yet trustworthy friends he closes his fickle lids.
Waiting for a new dawn, he admires the gift of nature with nothing to utter and plead.

The Ombud of Humanity

Life has fallen into a deep hole,
Humans are wearing & playing cutthroat.

Love is out for sale in the arcade,
Hatred is being procured in the cascade.

There I keep my head above all,
Avoiding the succumbs of territorial flaws.

As if the stars vouchsafed my accolade,
giving me solidity by being my colonnade.

I pledge to protect the rights of the populace,
scrutinizing, resolving the pickle at pace.

I will pull down the legs of dignified monsters,
dethroning them from the opulent bolster.

I accept being the ombud of humanity,
terminating the riff-raff of carcinogenicity.

The endless construct

Reality is the occurrence of dreams with the strongest sentiments.
Dreams form what we call reality.
All realities are once a dream.
Strong adhesion, efforts, and affection turn a dream into a reality.
What you learn and perceive fuels your imagination.
But dreams are not perceived rather they choose you
Due to some past accident or may, it be present coincidence or at times luck.
They occur naturally, never forced nor implanted.
If dreams are the base, then ideas represent the pillars.
The pillars hold the actions.
Actions are the roof sheltering successes and failures.
The more crushed your dreams are, the more creative you become.
Reality can never be crushed.
The more real you are, the less dreamy are your deeds.
Dreamers are gifted with the power to change the world.
But to change the world a dream must be lived.
So, to live a dream, risks are needed to be taken.
You need to have the guts to take risks.
Strong guts come from a focused vision and are analyzed before-works.

I miss people

I miss the people doing their daily chores,
I don't find them in crowded stores.
It's like a desert on the golden beaches,
There're no alarming security breaches.

I hardly see a new face,
Hesitantly ringing my doorbell.
I eagerly wait for my due days,
Fearing if my monthly pays fail.

I gaze upon the international news,
Trying to find a tint to fuse.
Netflix and chill are sounding so low,
Workout blogs moving my blood to flow.

I thrive on the peppy illogical memes,
Living inside the LCD screens.
I have lost the count of days,
The cherry & cream of the Sunday craze.

I praise the real heroes by lighting candles,

I hallow them through sounds and claps.
I seek a brighter day with shiny gift bundles,
I wait for the day when this epidemic lapses.

I notice the absence of the food trucks,
The delicious cheese on the pizza crusts.
I miss the gatherings and the traffic jams,
I wish to find them soon as a healthy clan.

Elixirs of Life

Life has certain rudiments that give proof of its liveliness
and they are the real elixir of life...
I have found a few risking my reach.
As the hour says "sharing is caring" and there's nothing
more daring to conclude such an ending.

The next pages will reveal the elixirs.
Hold your breath and drink all of it.

52

Hope- The 1st elixir.

Hope is the wind beneath our wings when we are afraid to fly. It lifts our spirit when we are low and calms our spirit. Hope is the glue that mends the heart that's broken now and then. And encourages the fallen to rise and try again.
Hope is the balm that soothes the pain when sorrows come to call, the anodyne that heals the heart and takes the fear away.
Hope is the star that leads the way throughout the silent life. Hope is the prayer that blesses the bliss all the time.
Life always has its ups and downs. For failures are never fatal as long as there is hope.

Determination- The 2nd elixir

A determination may take away your sleep for countless nights.

A determination may make you lose your appetite.

A determination may make you eremitic to a fraternity.

A determination may force you to run on lonely roads and desert you from your brotherhood.

A determination may tag you insane and call you a Tom o' Bedlam.

But in the end, it will definitely quench the thirst for your success which will overpower the cons owing to it.

Determination is the fuel that fires you perpetually to do something new and so strong, keeping you alive forever in the chronicles of time.

Luck- The 3rd elixir

Luck is capricious.
When it comes and goes nobody knows.
Luck is like a dice game whose results are whimsical.
Luck is a freshly released premier that never unveils what comes at the end.
Luck is a terra firma that can only be discovered by traveling through time.
Luck is a talisman only gifted to those who solve the mystery.
It's not our fate that creates luck but it is our deed that gives birth to it.
So, don't chase luck, go on doing your work, luck will definitely find you.

Motivation- The 4th elixir

Motivation is a catalyst that enhances the growth reaction of life.

Motivation is a ladder that escalates you to the top floor.

Motivation is the pole star that directs you to the north.

Motivation is an energized potion that accelerates your workability and empowers you.

Motivation is an adrenaline rush that gives you goosebumps and electrifies you.

Motivation levitates your thought and vocation beyond your limits.

These days' people of this kind are on the verge of extinction and a new trait of leg-pulling is dominating the era.

So, kill the crab instincts inside you and be a human.

There are many more hidden elixirs to unlock.

So keep searching and keep spreading.

Till my last breath

I love divergence
With no boundaries
No barriers
Fully stretched wings
In the infinite sky

Spoiling the ink
Of an eternal stylus
Pointy yet obtuse
Simple yet gorgeous
Cheap yet valuable

Give me a paper
And some ink
And I shall go on writing
Till my last breath.

Heart's recipe

Mystifying eyes
Sometimes candid
sometimes mystical,
For the eyes speak louder
Than the words blatantly literal.
Few crumbs of whites
Sprinkled on the passel of black.
That's what the heart is made with;
A pinch of good balancing
And an abundance of hell intact
So dive deeper and look closer
Explore yourself a hundred times
Who are you? - question further.

Past, Present and Future

Future is a thirst
Past is the quenched future,
And the present is the dilemma in between,
At times satisfaction and the rest with dereliction.
If your core is constructive enough
Then the value of your cladding doesn't matter much.

Acknowledgements

Gratitude is a colossal word and I would not let go of this beautiful opportunity to express it to the most deserving ones.

Firstly, my gratitude to the universe and life allowed me to experience a varsity of emotions and even feel nothing and blank for a while. I'd thank every such experience of mine that directly or indirectly has shaped me into the man I'm today.

I will thank my family, especially Maa and Papa, for forbearing every bit of my stubbornness and madness, being with me throughout my fluctuating phases, and supporting me to do my best. Thanks for believing in me.

I will also extend my gratitude to all the people as well as objects that brought the poet out of me, pulled my emotions through and through. Thanks to my friends for giving me many magical moments and bringing the tints of joy from time to time. Special thanks to my mirror without whom I wouldn't have viewed my real image.

Thanks to you, the readers, for buying the book and helping me to continue my writing journey. I hope my words emboss a positive impact on you. I would also ask you to share this with your loved ones.